CRUMB QUI|

Transform Scraps into Beautiful Quilts

BRANDON THORNE

Copyright © 2024

Table of contents

Introduction to Crumb Quilting
CHAPTER 1
    History and origin
    Applications of Crumb Quilting
    Materials and Tools
CHAPTER 2
    Basic Techniques
    Basic Crumb Piecing
    String Piecing
    Log Cabin Style Crumb Block
    Crumb Block with Fussy Cut Center
    Joining Crumb Blocks
CHAPTER 3
    Intermediate Techniques
    Crazy Quilt Blocks
    Improvisational Log Cabin Blocks
    Inset Circles or Curves
    Foundation Paper Piecing (FPP) with Scraps
    Creating a Scrappy Quilt-As-You-Go Block
CHAPTER 4
    Advanced Techniques
    Patchwork Mosaic
    Crumb Piecing with Applique
    Scrappy Quilt with Curved Piecing

Mixed Media Crumb Quilt

Free-Motion Quilting on Crumb Blocks

Tips for Success in Crumb Quilting

CHAPTER 5

Beginner project

Crumb Quilt Pillow Cover

Crumb Mug Rug

Crumb Coasters

Crumb Patchwork Tote Bag

Crumb Quilt Wall Hanging

CHAPTER 6

Intermediate Project

Crumb Quilt Table Runner

Crumb Quilt Wall Hanging with Applique

Crumb Quilt Baby Blanket

Crumb Quilt Tote Bag with Pockets

Crumb Quilt Throw Blanket

CHAPTER 7

Advanced project

Crumb Quilt Medallion Quilt

Crumb Quilt with Curved Piecing

Crumb Quilt with Inset Blocks

Crumb Quilt Landscape

Crumb Quilt T-shirt Memory Quilt

Troubleshooting and Solutions in Crumb
Quilting

Conclusion

Introduction to Crumb Quilting

Crumb quilting is a delightful and resourceful quilting technique that allows crafters to transform even the tiniest fabric scraps into beautiful, intricate quilts. This method is not only a fantastic way to use leftover materials, but it also offers endless opportunities for creativity and self-expression. Unlike traditional quilting, which often relies on precise patterns and uniform pieces, crumb quilting embraces irregularity and improvisation, making it an ideal project for quilters of all skill levels.

What is Crumb Quilting?

Crumb quilting involves piecing together small, often irregularly shaped scraps of fabric, known as "crumbs," to create unique quilt blocks. These scraps can be anything from leftover fabric strips and triangles to tiny bits that would typically be discarded. The process is similar to creating a patchwork collage, where each piece is sewn together with no strict rules or predefined patterns. The result is a vibrant, textured quilt that tells a story through its varied fabrics and colors.

The Appeal of Crumb Quilting

One of the most appealing aspects of crumb quilting is its accessibility. Because it doesn't require large pieces of fabric or precise cutting, it's perfect for those looking to start quilting without a big investment in materials. It's also an excellent way for seasoned quilters to use up their fabric stash and experiment with new ideas. The freeform nature of crumb quilting encourages experimentation and play, allowing quilters to explore different color combinations, textures, and designs without the pressure of following a pattern.

Eco-Friendly and Cost-Effective Crafting

In today's world, where sustainability is increasingly important, crumb quilting is an eco-friendly choice. It promotes the use of every bit of fabric, minimizing waste and maximizing the value of each piece. Even the smallest scraps, often considered unusable in other projects, find new life in crumb quilts. This thrifty approach not only reduces waste but also saves money, making it a budget-friendly hobby.

A Creative Outlet for All Skill Levels

Crumb quilting is a versatile technique that can be adapted to any skill level. For beginners, it provides a forgiving entry into the world of quilting, where mistakes are embraced as part of the process. There's no need to worry about precise measurements or matching seams perfectly—each block is unique, and imperfections add to the quilt's charm. For more experienced quilters, crumb quilting offers a chance to break away from traditional patterns and explore new artistic possibilities. The technique can be combined with other quilting methods, like paper piecing or appliqué, to create even more complex and stunning designs.

The Therapeutic Benefits of Crumb Quilting

Beyond the practical and creative aspects, crumb quilting is a meditative and therapeutic activity. The repetitive motions of piecing and sewing, combined with the freedom to create without strict guidelines, make it a relaxing and satisfying pastime. Many quilters find that working on a crumb quilt helps them unwind, focus, and express their emotions through fabric and color.

What You'll Learn in This Book

Whether you're a complete beginner or an experienced quilter looking to try something new, this book will guide you through the wonderful world of crumb quilting. You'll learn how to sort and prepare your scraps, piece them together into stunning blocks, and assemble your quilt top. We'll cover a range of techniques, from basic piecing to advanced design ideas, and explore various ways to finish and showcase your quilt. By the end of this journey, you'll have the skills and confidence to create your own crumb quilts, each one a unique reflection of your creativity and resourcefulness.

So, gather your scraps, thread your needle, and get ready to embark on a crumb quilting adventure. There's no correct method for making it happen — just your Let's turn those bits and pieces into something beautiful!

Difference Between Crumb Quilting and Other Quilting Techniques

Crumb quilting is a distinct and unique approach to quilt making that stands out from more traditional quilting techniques. While all quilting methods share the basic principles of piecing fabric together to create a quilt top, they differ in their methods, precision, and design philosophies. Here's a closer look at how crumb quilting differs from other popular quilting techniques:

1. **Precision vs. Improvisation**

- **Crumb Quilting**: This technique is all about improvisation and creativity. It involves piecing together small, often irregularly shaped scraps of fabric without strict guidelines or patterns. The focus is on creating a visually interesting and textured quilt top, with less emphasis on perfect seams or uniform shapes.

- **Traditional Quilting**: Most traditional quilting techniques require precision in cutting and piecing. Patterns such as log cabins, stars, and nine-patches rely on exact measurements and carefully cut fabric pieces to ensure that everything fits together perfectly. This precision is essential for maintaining the pattern's integrity and achieving a clean, polished look.

2. Use of Fabric Scraps

- **Crumb Quilting**: Crumb quilting embraces the use of even the tiniest scraps of fabric, often too small or oddly shaped for other quilting techniques. It's a perfect way to make use of leftover fabric bits, making it an eco-friendly and resourceful method.

- **Other Quilting Techniques**: While traditional quilting can also use scraps, it generally requires larger, more uniform pieces of fabric. Techniques like patchwork or appliqué often need specific shapes and sizes, which might limit the use of very small or irregularly shaped scraps.

3. Design Approach

- **Crumb Quilting**: The design process in crumb quilting is very freeform. Quilters build the quilt top by randomly adding pieces together, often without a preconceived plan. This spontaneous method results in unique, one-of-a-kind quilts where the overall design emerges organically as the project progresses.

- **Traditional Quilting**: Traditional quilting typically follows a pre-determined pattern or design.

Quilters choose a specific pattern, select fabrics that complement the design, and follow precise steps to achieve the desired outcome. There is less room for improvisation, as the goal is to replicate the chosen pattern as accurately as possible.

4. **Level of Structure**

- Crumb Quilting: There is very little structure in crumb quilting. Quilters are free to mix colors, fabrics, and patterns as they see fit. This lack of structure allows for greater experimentation but can also lead to a less cohesive final product if not balanced carefully.

- **Other Quilting Techniques**: Many traditional techniques have a high level of structure, with established rules for fabric placement, color harmony, and block arrangement. Techniques like paper piecing or foundation piecing provide a rigid framework that quilters follow to achieve precise results.

5. Quilt Blocks and Their Arrangement

- **Crumb Quilting**: Crumb blocks are typically made by piecing together small fabric scraps into larger blocks. These blocks can be any size and shape, and there's no need to match them with other blocks. Once the blocks are made, they are sewn together, often with additional borders or sashing, to form the quilt top.

- **Traditional Quilting**: In traditional quilting, blocks are usually created using specific patterns and then arranged in a grid to form the quilt top. The blocks need to be the same size and shape to fit together properly. The arrangement of the blocks often follows a specific pattern or layout to create a harmonious overall design.

6. Time and Complexity

- **Crumb Quilting**: The time and complexity of crumb quilting can vary widely. While piecing the scraps together is generally quick and easy, the lack of a predefined pattern can make it challenging to decide how to proceed. It's often a more relaxed process, allowing quilters to work at their own pace.

- **Other Quilting Techniques**: Traditional quilting patterns can range from simple to highly complex, often requiring careful planning, cutting, and piecing. Techniques like double wedding ring or Baltimore album quilts can take a long time to complete due to their intricate designs and the precision required.

7. Final Appearance and Style

- **Crumb Quilting**: The final appearance of a crumb quilt is often eclectic and vibrant, with a patchwork of different colors, patterns, and textures. It has a unique, artistic quality that reflects the quilter's personal style and creativity.

- **Other Quilting Techniques**: Traditional quilts often have a more uniform and cohesive look, with repeating patterns and balanced color schemes. They can range from classic and understated to complex and ornate, depending on the pattern and fabric choices.

In summary, crumb quilting is a liberating and creative technique that allows quilters to use every scrap of fabric in a spontaneous and unstructured way. Traditional quilting, on the other hand, is more structured and pattern-based, focusing on precision and symmetry. Both methods have their own charm and appeal, catering to different tastes and preferences within the quilting community.

CHAPTER 1

History and origin

Crumb quilting, as we know it today, has its roots in the broader tradition of patchwork and scrap quilting, techniques that have been practiced for centuries. While not as well-documented or formalized as some other quilting styles, crumb quilting has evolved as a nat.ural extension of the resourceful and creative spirit of quilters throughout history.

Early Beginnings of Scrap Quilting

The practice of using small, leftover pieces of fabric to create quilts dates back to the early days of quilting itself. In the 18th and 19th centuries, fabric was a precious commodity, and many households had limited resources. Quilters, especially in rural communities, would save every piece of fabric, no matter how small, to create warm bed coverings. This thrifty approach led to the creation of scrap quilts, where mismatched pieces were sewn together to form a quilt top. These quilts were often made out of necessity rather than for aesthetic reasons, reflecting the quilter's resourcefulness.

The Evolution into Crumb Quilting

The concept of crumb quilting emerged from this tradition of scrap quilting. The term "crumb" refers to the tiny, seemingly insignificant pieces of fabric that are often left over after cutting larger quilt blocks. These bits, sometimes as small as an inch or less, were traditionally seen as too small to be useful. However, quilters who were determined to waste nothing found ways to piece these small scraps together, creating blocks that, when assembled, produced a visually rich and textured quilt top.

This approach gained popularity in the 20th century, especially during the Great Depression of the 1930s, when resourcefulness was a necessity. Quilters made do with what they had, often incorporating fabrics from worn-out clothing, feed sacks, and other available textiles into their quilts. The resulting quilts were colorful and varied, reflecting the diverse fabrics used.

Modern Resurgence and Popularity

Crumb quilting, as a distinct technique, has experienced a resurgence in recent decades. With the rise of the modern quilting movement in the late 20th and early 21st centuries, quilters began to embrace a wider range of styles and techniques, including those that emphasized improvisation and creativity. The trend towards sustainability and the desire to minimize waste also contributed to the renewed interest in crumb quilting.

The internet and social media have played a significant role in spreading and popularizing crumb quilting. Online quilting communities, forums, and platforms like Pinterest and Instagram have allowed quilters to share their creations and inspire others. Tutorials, blog posts, and YouTube videos have made it easier for quilters of all skill levels to learn and experiment with this technique.

The Philosophy Behind Crumb Quilting

Crumb quilting embodies a philosophy of making the most of what is available. It celebrates the beauty in imperfection and the uniqueness of each quilt. Unlike traditional quilting, which often follows strict patterns and guidelines, crumb quilting encourages quilters to let go of rigid expectations and embrace a more freeform, spontaneous approach. This mindset is not just about quilting; it reflects a broader creative attitude of using what you have and finding value in what might otherwise be discarded.

Crumb Quilting in Contemporary Quilt Art

In recent years, crumb quilting has found a place in contemporary quilt art, with artists and quilters using the technique to explore themes of memory, resourcefulness, and sustainability. These quilts often go beyond the functional, serving as visual narratives or expressions of the quilter's personal history and artistic vision.

Many quilters now see crumb quilting as a way to connect with the past while also pushing the boundaries of what a quilt can be. By piecing together the smallest scraps, they create something greater than the sum of its parts—a quilt that is not only visually striking but also rich in meaning and history.

The history and origin of crumb quilting are deeply rooted in the broader tradition of quilting as an art of necessity and creativity. From its humble beginnings in scrap and patchwork quilting to its modern resurgence as a celebrated and sustainable technique, crumb quilting has always been about making the most of what you have and finding beauty in the unexpected. Today, it continues to evolve and inspire quilters around the world, embodying a timeless spirit of resourcefulness and artistic expression.

Applications of Crumb Quilting

Crumb quilting is a versatile technique that lends itself to a wide range of creative projects beyond traditional bed quilts. Its improvisational nature and use of small fabric scraps make it perfect for crafting unique and eye-catching items that can be both practical and decorative. Here are some popular applications of crumb quilting:

1. Traditional Quilts

- **Bed Quilts**: Crumb quilts make for cozy, colorful bed covers. They can range from small, crib-sized quilts to large king-sized bedspreads. The patchwork of varied fabrics adds warmth and visual interest to any bedroom decor.

- **Lap Quilts and Throws**: Smaller than bed quilts, lap quilts and throws are ideal for keeping warm on the couch or as decorative accents. They're a perfect way to showcase crumb quilting on a smaller scale.

2. Home Décor Items

- **Pillow Covers**: Crumb quilt blocks can be used to make vibrant and textured pillow covers. These pillows add a splash of color and personality to sofas, chairs, and beds.

- **Table Runners and Placemats**: Crumb quilted table runners and placemats bring a unique, handmade touch to dining tables. They can be tailored to fit any table size and easily customized to match the season or occasion.

- **Wall Hangings and Art Quilts**: Crumb quilting can be used to create intricate wall hangings and art quilts. These pieces can serve as a focal point in a room, showcasing the quilter's creativity and artistic vision.

3. Personal Accessories

- **Bags and Pouches**: Crumb quilting is perfect for making bags, tote bags, pouches, and purses. The quilted fabric adds durability and texture, while the patchwork design makes each bag a one-of-a-kind statement piece.

- **Notebook Covers**: Quilted fabric covers for notebooks or journals are a unique way to personalize stationery. They also make thoughtful gifts for writers, artists, or anyone who loves to journal.

4. **Gift Items**

- **Baby Quilts**: Crumb quilting is ideal for making baby quilts, which can be given as special, handmade gifts for new parents. The colorful and playful nature of crumb quilting suits a variety of baby themes.

- **Memory Quilts**: Crumb quilting can be used to create memory quilts by incorporating pieces of clothing, fabric from special occasions, or even sentimental items like baby clothes or uniforms. These quilts serve as keepsakes, preserving cherished memories in a beautiful, functional form.

- **Mug Rugs and Coasters**: Smaller crumb quilt projects like mug rugs (miniature placemats) and coasters are quick and easy to make. They are perfect for using up even the smallest scraps and make great gifts or craft fair items.

5. Upcycling and Repurposing

- **Clothing Remakes**: Crumb quilting can be used to patch or embellish clothing. It's a creative way to repair or refresh old jeans, jackets, or bags, giving them a new lease on life with a personalized touch.

- **Scrap Management**: For quilters with large fabric stashes, crumb quilting is an effective way to manage and reduce fabric waste. By turning even the smallest pieces into something beautiful, it helps keep the sewing space organized and sustainable.

6. Seasonal and Themed Projects

- **Holiday Décor**: Crumb quilting is perfect for making holiday-themed items like Christmas stockings, tree skirts, or Easter table runners. By selecting scraps in seasonal colors or prints, quilters can create festive, handmade décor.

- **Themed Quilts**: Crumb quilting can be adapted to fit any theme, whether it's a favorite color scheme, a hobby, or a particular season. Themed quilts can be great for personalized gifts or special occasions.

7. Quilt Alongs and Community Projects

- **Quilt Alongs**: Many online quilting communities host quilt-along events, where participants create quilts based on a shared theme or pattern. Crumb quilting lends itself well to these projects, as it allows for individual creativity within a group activity.

- **Charity Quilts**: Crumb quilts are an excellent choice for charity quilting projects. The quick and resourceful nature of crumb quilting means that quilters can produce beautiful, functional quilts to donate to those in need.

8. Teaching and Learning

- **Beginner Projects**: Crumb quilting is a fantastic way to teach beginners the basics of piecing and sewing without the pressure of precision cutting and matching. It's a forgiving technique that allows new quilters to build confidence.

- **Technique Demonstrations**: For experienced quilters, crumb quilting can be a fun technique to teach at workshops, classes, or quilt guild meetings. It introduces a creative, low-stress approach to quilting that can inspire participants to try something new.

In summary, crumb quilting's versatility and resourcefulness make it applicable to a wide range of projects, from traditional quilts to innovative home décor and accessories. Its adaptability allows quilters to use every scrap of fabric creatively, resulting in beautiful and unique handmade items that can be cherished for years.

Materials and Tools

Crumb quilting is a flexible and resourceful technique that doesn't require specialized tools or materials. Most quilters will already have the necessary items in their sewing stash, making it an accessible and budget-friendly craft. Below is a comprehensive list of the essential materials and tools needed for crumb quilting.

Essential Materials

1. **Fabric Scraps**:
   - **Crumbs**: The cornerstone of crumb quilting is small fabric scraps, often referred to as "crumbs." These can be any leftover pieces from previous quilting projects, including irregular shapes, strips, and small squares.

   - **Variety of Fabrics**: Use a mix of cottons, prints, solids, and even novelty fabrics to add interest and texture to your quilt. Avoid using fabrics that fray easily, like loosely woven materials, as they can be challenging to work with.

   - **Coordinating Fabrics**: Although crumb quilting is all about variety, having a few coordinating fabrics can help tie your quilt together. Consider using a solid or a repeating color to create visual cohesion.

2. **Foundation Fabric (Optional)**:

Some quilters prefer to use a foundation fabric, such as muslin or lightweight cotton, to stitch the crumbs onto. This can provide stability and help keep small pieces from shifting. It's optional but recommended for beginners.

3. **Thread**:

Use a good-quality cotton thread that complements your fabric colors. Unbiased varieties like beige, dim, or white are flexible decisions. For added interest, consider using contrasting thread to highlight your stitching.

4. **Quilt Batting**:

Quilt batting provides the inner layer of the quilt, adding warmth and structure. Cotton or polyester batting works well, depending on your preference for loft and weight.

5. **Backing Fabric**:

Choose a fabric for the quilt back that complements the front. It can be a solid color, a simple print, or even pieced scraps for a fully reversible quilt.

6. **Binding Fabric**:

The limiting is the texture strip that completes the edges of the blanket. Choose a fabric that compliments your quilt top or use leftover crumbs for a scrappy binding.

Essential Tools

1. **Sewing Machine**:

A standard sewing machine with a quarter-inch foot (for seam allowances) is ideal for piecing crumb blocks. Ensure your machine is in good working order, as crumb quilting involves a lot of piecing and sewing.

2. **Rotary Cutter and Cutting Mat:**

A rotary cutter and self-healing cutting mat are essential for trimming fabric pieces and straightening edges. A small rotary cutter (28mm) can be helpful for cutting small scraps, while a larger one (45mm) is great for trimming blocks.

3. **Quilting Ruler:**

A clear acrylic ruler is necessary for cutting and trimming fabric. A smaller ruler (6.5" x 12.5") is handy for working with crumb blocks, while a larger one (6.5" x 24") is useful for trimming larger pieces.

4. **Iron and Ironing Board**:

- Pressing your fabric and seams is crucial in quilting. An iron and ironing board help to press seams open or to one side, making your blocks flatter and easier to work with.

5. **Pins or Clips:**

Use pins or fabric clips to hold small pieces in place while sewing. They help maintain accuracy, especially when working with tiny or irregular scraps.

6. **Seam Ripper**:

Mistakes happen, and a seam ripper is essential for undoing stitches without damaging the fabric.

7. **Fabric Scissors**:

Good quality fabric scissors are important for cutting fabric accurately. Keep them sharp and separate from other scissors to avoid dulling the blades.

8. **Marking Tools**:

A fabric marker or chalk pencil can be helpful for marking seam lines or cutting lines, especially when working with irregularly shaped scraps.

9. **Spray Starch (Optional):**

Spray starch can be used to stiffen fabrics and make them easier to work with. It's especially useful for stabilizing lightweight or stretchy fabrics.

Additional Tools for Quilting and Finishing

1. Walking Foot (for Quilting):

A walking foot helps feed multiple layers of fabric evenly through the sewing machine, preventing puckering or shifting while quilting.

2. Quilting Needles:

Use sharp, quilting-specific needles for both your sewing machine and hand quilting (if desired). Size 80/12 or 90/14 needles work well for most quilting cottons.

3. Basting Pins or Spray:

Basting is necessary to hold the quilt layers together before quilting. Use curved safety pins or basting spray to secure the quilt sandwich.

4. Quilting Gloves (Optional):

Quilting gloves with rubberized fingertips provide better grip and control when quilting larger projects.

Storage and Organization

1. **Scrap Bins or Containers**:

Keep your fabric scraps organized by size or color in separate bins or containers. This makes it easier to find the pieces you need when creating your crumb blocks.

2. **Thread Organizer**:

An organizer for your threads helps keep them tangle-free and accessible, especially if you're using multiple colors in your project.

Crumb quilting is a flexible and accessible technique that doesn't require much beyond the basics most quilters already have. With a variety of scraps, basic sewing tools, and a willingness to experiment, you can create stunning, unique quilts that showcase your creativity and resourcefulness. Whether you're a beginner or an experienced quilter, having the right materials and tools will make your crumb quilting journey both enjoyable and successful.

CHAPTER 2

Basic Techniques

Crumb quilting is a creative and improvisational technique that allows quilters to use even the smallest fabric scraps to create unique and vibrant quilts. Below, you'll find the essential materials needed, followed by a step-by-step guide to five basic crumb quilting techniques.

Materials Needed

1. **Fabric Scraps**: A variety of small fabric pieces, often called "crumbs," including odd shapes, strips, and small squares. Any cotton fabric works well, but you can experiment with different textures and prints.

2. **Thread**: Good-quality cotton or polyester thread in a neutral color like white, gray, or beige. You can also use colorful or contrasting thread for a decorative effect.

3. **Sewing Machine**: A standard sewing machine with a quarter-inch foot for accurate seam allowances. A basic machine is sufficient for piecing crumb blocks.

4. **Rotary Cutter, Cutting Mat, and Quilting Ruler**: A rotary cutter (preferably 28mm for small pieces), a self-healing cutting mat, and a clear quilting ruler for cutting and trimming fabric.

5. **Iron and Ironing Board**: An iron is essential for pressing seams and fabric scraps flat, which helps in achieving a smooth quilt top.

6. **Pins or Clips**: Use pins or fabric clips to hold pieces together while sewing, especially for tiny or irregular scraps.

7. **Seam Ripper**: A seam ripper is handy for correcting mistakes or reworking seams.

Basic Crumb Piecing

Step-by-Step guide:

1. **Choose Your Scraps**:

   - Select two small fabric scraps that you would like to join. These can be any shape or size.

2. **Sew the First Seam:**

- Place the two fabric pieces right sides together along one edge. Sew a quarter-inch seam along this edge.

3. **Press the Seam**:

- Use your iron to press the seam open or to one side. This will help the pieces lie flat and make the next step easier.

4. **Add More Scraps**:

- Continue adding small scraps to the piece you've created. Align the scraps' edges, sew them together with a quarter-inch seam, and press after each addition. Keep adding scraps until you have a small patchwork piece (around 4 to 6 inches).

5. **Trim the Block**:

- Once your crumb piece reaches the desired size, use your rotary cutter and quilting ruler to trim it into a square or rectangular shape. Repeat this process to make multiple crumb blocks.

String Piecing

Step-by-Step guide:

1. Foundation Fabric (Optional):

- Cut a piece of foundation fabric, such as muslin, to the size you want your final block to be. This is optional but helps stabilize your pieces.

2. Arrange Fabric Strips:

- Choose narrow fabric strips (about 1 to 2 inches wide) from your scrap collection. Place the first strip right side up diagonally across the foundation fabric.

3. **Add the Next Strip**:

- Place a second strip right sides together on top of the first strip, aligning the edges. Sew along the aligned edge with a quarter-inch seam.

4. **Press and Continue**:

- Press the second strip open, then add another strip in the same manner. Continue adding strips until the entire foundation is covered.

5. **Trim the Block**:
- Use a rotary cutter and ruler to trim the edges of the block to the size of the foundation piece, creating a neat, finished block.

Log Cabin Style Crumb Block

Step-by-Step guide:

1. Start with a Center Piece:

- Choose a small square or rectangle to use as the center of your block.

2. Add First Round of Strips:

- Select a strip of fabric and sew it to one side of the center piece, right sides together. Press the seam.

3. **Add the Next Strip**:

- Sew another strip to the adjacent side of the block, continuing in a clockwise or counter-clockwise direction. Press after each addition.

4. **Continue Building**:
- Keep adding strips around the block in a log cabin style until you reach the desired size.

5. **Trim the Block**:

- Trim the edges to square up the block, ensuring all sides are even.

Crumb Block with Fussy Cut Center

Step-by-Step guide:

1. Select a Fussy Cut Piece:

- Choose a fabric piece with a distinct motif (e.g., a flower or animal) and cut it out, leaving a small border around the design.

2. **Add Crumb Pieces**:

- Begin adding small crumb pieces around the fussy cut center. Sew a piece to one side, press, then add another piece to an adjacent side.

3. **Build Outward**:

- Continue adding crumbs, expanding out from the center. Keep sewing and pressing until the block reaches your desired size.

4. **Trim the Block**:

- Use a rotary cutter and ruler to trim the block into a neat square or rectangle.

5. **Frame the Center**:

- If desired, add a border or frame around the fussy cut center using longer strips of fabric to emphasize the motif.

Joining Crumb Blocks

Step-by-Step guide:

1. **Arrange the Blocks**:

- Lay out your crumb blocks on a flat surface to decide on the arrangement. Consider color and pattern distribution.

2. Sew the Blocks Together:

- Place two blocks right sides together and sew along one edge with a quarter-inch seam. Repeat to create rows of blocks.

3. Join the Rows:

- Sew the rows together, matching seams where possible. Press the seams open or to one side.

4. Add Sashing (Optional):
- If you want to separate your crumb blocks with sashing, cut strips of fabric and sew them between the blocks and rows before joining them.

5. Complete the Quilt Top:

- Once all blocks and sashing are joined, your quilt top is complete. You can now layer it with batting and backing fabric, quilt as desired, and finish with binding.

These basic techniques provide a foundation for creating beautiful crumb quilts. With the right materials and a willingness to experiment, you can turn even the smallest fabric scraps into stunning quilt projects!

CHAPTER 3

Intermediate Techniques

As you advance in crumb quilting, you can explore more complex designs and incorporate additional techniques to elevate your projects. Below are five intermediate crumb quilting techniques, each requiring specific materials and tools to enhance your creative process.

Materials Needed

1. **Fabric Scraps**: A large variety of fabric scraps in different sizes, shapes, colors, and patterns. Include some medium-sized pieces (around 4 to 6 inches) for more complex blocks.

2. **Coordinating Fabric**: Solid or tonal fabrics that complement your scraps. These can be used to create borders, frames, or sashing within your blocks.

3. **Thread**: High-quality cotton or polyester thread in neutral colors for piecing. You can also use variegated or contrasting thread for decorative stitching.

4. **Sewing Machine**: A standard sewing machine with a quarter-inch foot. An optional walking foot may be useful for quilting thicker layers.

5. **Rotary Cutter, Cutting Mat, and Quilting Ruler**: Essential for precise cutting and trimming. A square ruler (6.5" x 6.5") is useful for squaring up blocks, while a larger ruler (6.5" x 24") is good for cutting strips.

6. **Iron and Ironing Board**: A must-have for pressing seams between steps to keep your blocks flat and neat.

7. **Pins or Clips**: For holding pieces together while you sew, especially when working with curves or complex seams.

8. **Foundation Fabric (Optional)**: Lightweight cotton or muslin can be used for added stability when working with intricate blocks.

9. **Templates (Optional)**: Plastic or cardboard templates for cutting precise shapes, such as triangles, hexagons, or circles.

10. **Quilting Supplies**: Quilt batting, backing fabric, and binding material for finishing your quilt.

Crazy Quilt Blocks

Step-by-Step Guide:

1. **Create a Foundation (Optional):**

   - Cut a square or rectangle of foundation fabric to the desired size of your finished block.

2. **Select a Center Piece**:

- Choose an irregular scrap to start. Place it in the center of the foundation fabric (if using one).

3. **Add Irregular Shapes**:

- Select irregular scraps and sew them around the center piece. Place each piece right sides together with an adjacent side of the center, sew a seam, and press.

4. **Continue Adding Pieces**:

- Keep adding pieces in a clockwise or counter-clockwise direction. Vary the shapes and angles of the pieces to create a "crazy" patchwork look.

5. **Trim the Block**:

- Once the block is fully covered, use your rotary cutter and ruler to trim it to a uniform size.

Improvisational Log Cabin Blocks

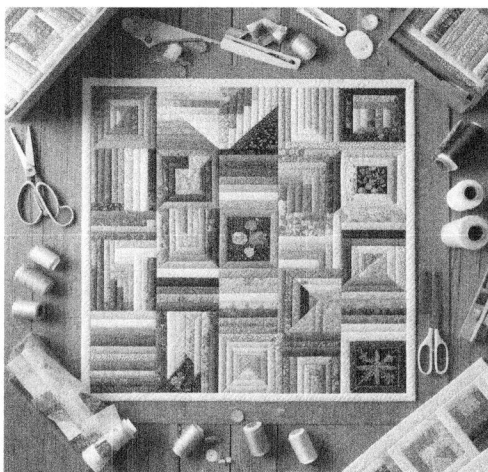

Step by step guide:

1. **Choose a Center Piece**:

   - Start with a square or rectangle center piece, but use a scrap with an irregular or off-center shape for added interest.

2. **Add Log Cabin Strips**:

   - Sew strips around the center piece, one side at a time. Use scraps of varying widths and lengths to create a wonky or asymmetrical effect.

3. **Vary the Strip Widths**:

- Use strips of different widths and angles to build your block outward, giving it a freeform, improvisational look.

4. **Continue Building**:
- Keep adding strips until the block reaches the desired size, adjusting the angles and widths as you go.

5. **Trim and Square Up**:

- Use your ruler to trim the block into a neat square or rectangle.

Inset Circles or Curves

Step by step guide:

1. Create Templates:

   - Use plastic or cardboard templates to cut circles or curved shapes from your scraps.

2. **Cut Background Fabric**:

   - Cut a square of background fabric larger than your circle. Cut a matching circle from the center of the background fabric.

3. **Sew the Circle**:

- Pin the circle into the cut-out hole in the background fabric, aligning the edges. Use lots of pins or clips to keep the pieces in place.

4. **Sew Carefully**:

- Slowly sew around the edge of the circle with a quarter-inch seam, easing the fabric to avoid puckers.

5. **Press and Trim**:

- Press the seam and trim the block to the desired size.

Foundation Paper Piecing (FPP) with Scraps

Step by step guide:

1. **Prepare the Paper Pattern**:

   - Print or draw a simple block pattern on lightweight paper. Basic designs like stars, trees, or geometric shapes work well.

2. **Position the First Scrap**:

   - Place the first scrap on the back of the paper, right side facing out. Make sure it covers the first section of the pattern with a generous seam allowance.

3. **Add the Next Piece**:

- Place the next scrap right sides together with the first, aligning with the seam line on the pattern. Sew along the line on the printed side of the paper.

4. **Trim and Press**:

- Flip the fabric over and press. Trim excess fabric, leaving a quarter-inch seam allowance.

5. **Continue Building**:

- Repeat with additional scraps until the entire pattern is covered. Carefully tear away the paper backing once the block is complete.

Creating a Scrappy Quilt-As-You-Go Block

Step by step guide

1. **Cut Batting and Backing**:

   - Cut a square of quilt batting and backing fabric to the desired block size.

2. **Start with a Center Scrap**:

- Place a scrap in the center of the batting. Pin or baste it in place.

3. **Add Surrounding Pieces**:

- Sew additional scraps around the center piece, similar to log cabin construction. Sew through all layers (scrap, batting, and backing) as you go.

4. **Quilt Each Piece:**

- Use decorative stitches or straight-line quilting to quilt each piece as you add it, securing it to the batting and backing.

5. **Trim and Join Blocks**:
- Trim each block to the desired size and join them together using sashing strips or by sewing them directly, joining batting and backing layers at the same time.

These intermediate techniques will help you create more complex and visually striking crumb quilts. With the right materials and a little practice, you'll be able to expand your skills and create unique quilts that reflect your personal style and creativity.

CHAPTER 4

Advanced Techniques

Once you have mastered the basics and intermediate techniques of crumb quilting, you can dive into advanced methods that incorporate complex designs, specialized skills, and innovative techniques. Below are five advanced crumb quilting techniques, along with the necessary materials to execute them effectively.

Materials Needed

1. **Fabric Scraps**: A wide variety of fabric scraps, including larger pieces (6 inches or more), specialty fabrics (like silks or flannels), and textured materials for added depth.

2. **Coordinating and Accent Fabrics**: Solid and printed fabrics to be used for borders, sashing, or as focal points within your design.

3. **Thread**: High-quality cotton or polyester thread, with options for specialty threads like metallics or variegated colors for decorative stitching.

4. **Sewing Machine**: A reliable sewing machine with multiple stitch options, including a walking foot for better handling of layers during quilting.

5. **Rotary Cutter, Cutting Mat, and Quilting Ruler**: Essential tools for precise cutting and trimming. A square ruler (6.5" x 6.5") and larger rulers (6.5" x 24") are helpful for various sizes of blocks.

6. **Iron and Ironing Board**: For pressing seams and fabric scraps to achieve a professional finish.

7. **Pins or Clips**: For securely holding layers and fabric pieces while sewing, especially important in complex designs.

8. **Foundation Fabric or Specialty Stabilizers**:

Lightweight cotton or specialized stabilizers for specific techniques like embroidery or delicate fabrics.

9. **Templates**: Plastic or cardboard templates for cutting precise shapes (triangles, hexagons, or curves).

10. **Quilting Supplies**: Quilt batting, backing fabric, and binding material for finishing your quilt.

11. **Embellishment Supplies (Optional)**: Beads, buttons, lace, or other embellishments to add texture and design interest.

Patchwork Mosaic

Step by step procedure:

1. Choose Your Fabrics:

- Select a range of fabric scraps that you'd like to use to create a mosaic effect. Consider different colors, patterns, and textures.

2. Cut Small Pieces:

- Use your rotary cutter and ruler to cut the fabric scraps into small squares or rectangles, ideally measuring 1 to 2 inches.

3. **Design Your Mosaic**:

- Lay out your squares on a design wall or flat surface, arranging them into a mosaic pattern. Experiment with color placement and design until you're satisfied.

4. **Sew the Squares Together**:

- Begin sewing the squares together in rows, using a quarter-inch seam allowance. Press the seams open after sewing each row.

5. **Join the Rows**:

- After completing the rows, sew them together to create your final mosaic block. Trim any uneven edges for a clean finish.

Crumb Piecing with Applique

Step by step procedure:

1. **Create a Background Block:**

   - Start by making a background crumb block using your typical crumb piecing method.
2. **Choose Applique Shapes**:

- Cut out fabric shapes or motifs from scraps or coordinating fabrics for appliqué. These can be flowers, leaves, animals, or abstract designs.

3. **Prepare for Applique**:

- If desired, use fusible web to attach the appliqué shapes to the background. This helps stabilize the pieces before sewing.

4. **Sew the Appliqué**:

- Use a zigzag or decorative stitch to sew around the edges of the appliqué shapes, securing them to the background. You can also use hand-stitching for a more textured look.

5. **Finish the Block**:

- Trim the background block to your desired size. Add any additional embellishments, like embroidery or beads, for a unique touch.

Scrappy Quilt with Curved Piecing

Step by step procedure

1. **Select Your Fabrics**:

- Choose a variety of fabric scraps, focusing on pieces that can create interesting shapes.

2. **Create Templates for Curves**:

- Use cardboard or plastic to create templates for the curved shapes you wish to sew. Common shapes include arcs, circles, or waves.

3. **Cut the Fabric**:

- Use the templates to cut out the curved shapes from your fabric scraps.

4. **Sewing Curved Seams**:

- Pin the curved pieces together, ensuring the edges align. Sew slowly, easing the fabric as you go to prevent puckering.

5. **Press and Trim**:

- Press the seams open or to one side. Trim the block to a uniform size and incorporate it into your quilt design.

Mixed Media Crumb Quilt

Step by step procedure:

1. Gather Materials:

- In addition to fabric scraps, collect non-traditional materials such as lace, felt, or paper for mixed media effects.

2. Design Your Layout:

- Lay out your fabric scraps and non-fabric materials on a design wall. Experiment with layering and placement until you have a composition you like.

3. **Sew the Layers**:

- Begin by sewing your fabric scraps together to form a block. Incorporate the non-fabric materials by layering them over the fabric and stitching through all layers.

4. **Add Embellishments**:

- Use decorative stitching or hand embroidery to enhance the mixed media elements and secure everything in place.

5. **Finish Your Block**:

- Trim and square up the block as needed. Assemble the blocks into a quilt top and proceed to quilt as desired.

Free-Motion Quilting on Crumb Blocks

Step by step procedure:

1. **Prepare Your Quilt Sandwich:**

- Layer your crumb blocks with batting and backing fabric to create a quilt sandwich. Treat or pin to keep the layers intact.

2. **Set Up for Free-Motion Quilting**:

- Attach a darning foot or free-motion foot to your sewing machine and lower the feed dogs. Pick a string that supplements your texture.

3. **Practice Free-Motion Stitches**:

- Before starting on the quilt, practice free-motion stitches on scrap fabric to get comfortable with movement and design.

4. **Quilt Your Crumb Blocks**:
- Begin free-motion quilting on your crumb blocks. Move the fabric under the needle to create intricate patterns, swirls, or motifs.

5. **Finish the Quilting**:

- Once you have quilted all your blocks, trim any excess batting and backing. Add restricting to complete the edges of your blanket.

These advanced techniques allow you to push the boundaries of crumb quilting, integrating various methods and materials to create unique, artistic quilt designs. With practice and creativity, you can develop your style and make stunning quilts that showcase your skills and vision.

Tips for Success in Crumb Quilting

Crumb quilting is a rewarding and creative process that encourages experimentation and personal expression. Here are some tips to help you achieve success in your crumb quilting projects:

1. **Embrace Imperfection**:

- One of the joys of crumb quilting is its improvisational nature. Don't worry about achieving perfectly aligned seams or matching points. Embrace the beauty of randomness and the unique character of each piece.

2. **Organize Your Scraps**:

- Keep your fabric scraps organized by size, color, or type. This makes it easier to find the right pieces when you start a new project and can inspire creative combinations.

3. **Experiment with Color and Texture**:

- Play with different colors, prints, and textures to create visually interesting quilts. Use contrasting fabrics to make certain elements pop or experiment with similar shades for a more subtle effect.

4. **Use a Design Wall**:

- A design wall allows you to lay out your pieces and visualize the overall composition before sewing. This can help you rearrange blocks or colors until you achieve the desired look.

5. **Practice Your Techniques**:

- Take time to practice different techniques on scrap fabric before applying them to your main project. This helps build your skills and confidence, especially for more complex methods.

6. **Incorporate Different Techniques:**

- Combine crumb quilting with other quilting techniques, such as appliqué, foundation piecing, or free-motion quilting. Mixing techniques adds depth and interest to your projects.

7. **Keep Your Tools Handy**:

- Ensure you have all necessary tools—scissors, rotary cutter, ruler, pins, and thread—within reach when working on your projects. This will keep your workflow efficient and enjoyable.

8. **Press Frequently**:

- Press seams as you go to keep your blocks flat and neat. This also helps in aligning pieces more accurately during assembly.

9. **Take Breaks:**

- Quilting can be a time-consuming task, so remember to take breaks to avoid fatigue. Stepping away can also provide fresh perspective when you return to your project.

10. **Join a Quilting Community**:
   - Engage with other quilters, whether in person or online. Sharing ideas, tips, and inspiration can motivate you and enhance your quilting skills.

11. **Document Your Process**:

   - Keep a diary or take photographs of your advancement. This allows you to reflect on your creative journey and track your development as a quilter.

12. **Have Fun**:

   - Enjoy the process! Crumb quilting is meant to be a creative outlet, so let your imagination run wild and don't stress about the end result.

By following these tips, you can enhance your crumb quilting experience, improve your skills, and create beautiful, unique quilts that reflect your personal style and creativity. Happy quilting!

CHAPTER 5

Beginner project

Starting your journey in crumb quilting can be both fun and rewarding. Here are five beginner-friendly projects, complete with the necessary materials and step-by-step instructions.

Crumb Quilt Pillow Cover

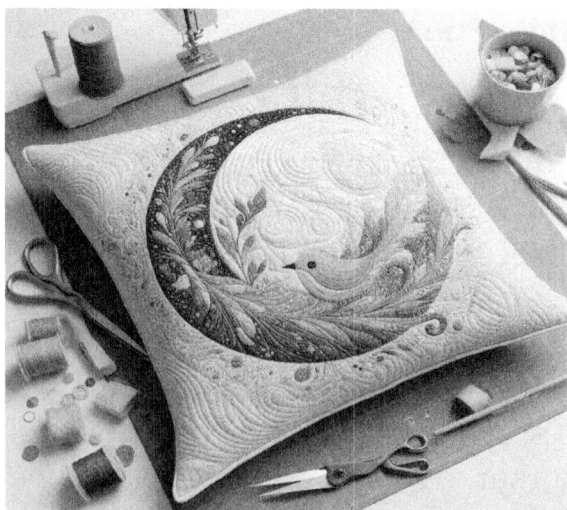

Materials Needed:

1. Fabric scraps (various sizes)
2. Muslin or plain cotton for backing
3. Batting (optional)
4. Thread (matching or contrasting)
5. Sewing machine
6. Rotary cutter, cutting mat, and quilting ruler
7. Iron and ironing board
8. Pillow insert (standard size)

Steps:

1. **Create the Crumb Block**: Start by sewing together your fabric scraps to form a block at least 16" x 16". Utilize various sizes and shapes for a powerful look.

2. **Trim the Block**: Once the block is complete, trim it to 16" x 16" using your rotary cutter and ruler.

3. **Prepare the Backing**: Cut a piece of muslin or plain cotton to the same size as your block (16" x 16").

4. **Layer the Pillow Cover**: If using batting, layer it underneath the crumb block and place the backing on the back (right sides together).

5. **Sew the Edges**: Sew around the edges, leaving a small opening (about 4-5 inches) for turning.

6. **Turn and Press**: Turn the pillow cover right side out and press flat.

7. **Insert Pillow**: Insert your pillow insert into the cover and hand-sew the opening closed.

Crumb Mug Rug

Materials Needed:

1. Fabric scraps (smaller pieces)

2. Batting (8" x 10" piece)

3. Thread (matching or contrasting)

4. Sewing machine.

5. Rotary cutter, cutting mat, and quilting ruler

6. Iron and ironing board

Steps:

1. **Create the Crumb Top**: Sew together scraps to create a top piece measuring approximately 8" x 10".

2. Prepare the Batting: Cut the batting to 8" x 10".

3. **Layer the Mug Rug**: Layer the crumb top over the batting.

4. **Quilt the Mug Rug**: Use your sewing machine to quilt the layers together. Straight lines or free-motion designs can work well.

5. **Trim and Bind**: Trim any excess batting and fabric to ensure the edges are even. Add a simple binding around the edges if desired.

Crumb Coasters

Materials Needed:

1. Fabric scraps (small pieces)

2. Batting (cut into 4" x 4" squares)

3. Thread (matching or contrasting)

4. Sewing machine

5. Rotary cutter, cutting mat, and quilting ruler

6. Iron and ironing board

Steps:

1. **Create the Crumb Top**: Sew scraps together to form a block of at least 5" x 5" for each coaster.

2. **Cut the Coasters**: Cut the crumb block into four 4" x 4" squares.

3. **Layer the Coasters**: Layer each crumb square on a piece of batting.

4. **Quilt the Coasters**: Quilt each coaster as desired, either with straight lines or free-motion quilting.

5. **Finish the Edges**: Trim any excess batting and finish the edges with a zigzag stitch or binding if desired.

Crumb Patchwork Tote Bag

Materials Needed:

1. Fabric scraps (various sizes)

2. Muslin or cotton for lining

3. Thread (matching or contrasting)

4. Sewing machine

5. Rotary cutter, cutting mat, and quilting ruler

6. Iron and ironing board

7. Straps (fabric or webbing)

Steps:

1. **Create the Tote Front**: Sew together fabric scraps to create a large block measuring approximately 12" x 18".

2. **Prepare the Lining**: Cut a piece of lining fabric the same size as the front.

3. **Make the Straps**: Cut two pieces of fabric or webbing for straps, each about 1.5" wide and 18" long.

4. **Assemble the Tote**: Place the crumb block and lining right sides together, inserting the straps at the top edges.

5. **Sew and Turn**: Sew around the edges, leaving the top open. Turn the bag right side out.

6. **Finish the Top Edge**: Press the top edge and topstitch for a finished look.

Crumb Quilt Wall Hanging

Materials Needed:

1. Fabric scraps (various sizes)

2. Batting (optional)

3. Thread (matching or contrasting)

4. Sewing machine
5. Rotary cutter, cutting mat, and quilting ruler

6. Iron and ironing board

7. Hanging rod or dowel

Steps:

1. Create the Crumb Block: Sew fabric scraps together to form a larger block, ideally around 24" x 36".

2. **Prepare Backing**: Cut a piece of fabric for backing that matches your block size.

3. **Layer the Wall Hanging**: Layer the crumb block over the backing (add batting if desired).

4. **Quilt the Layers**: Quilt through all layers using straight or decorative stitches.

5. **Finish the Edges**: Trim any excess fabric and finish the edges with binding or by folding over the back.

6. **Attach Hanging Rod**: Create a pocket at the top of the wall hanging for a rod or dowel to display.

These beginner projects provide a great starting point for your crumb quilting journey, allowing you to practice your skills while creating functional and beautiful items. Enjoy your quilting adventure!

CHAPTER 6

Intermediate Project

Once you've mastered the basics of crumb quilting, you can take on intermediate projects that involve more complex techniques and designs. Here are five intermediate projects, complete with the necessary materials and step-by-step instructions.

Crumb Quilt Table Runner

Materials Needed:

1. Fabric scraps (various sizes)
2. Muslin or cotton fabric for backing

3. Batting (optional)

4. Thread (matching or contrasting)

5. Sewing machine

6. Rotary cutter, cutting mat, and quilting ruler

7. Iron and ironing board

8. Binding fabric

Steps:
1. **Create Crumb Blocks**: Sew together fabric scraps to create several blocks, each measuring 6" x 12". Aim for at least three to five blocks for a table runner.

2. **Trim the Blocks**: After piecing, trim each block to ensure they are uniform in size.

3. **Arrange the Blocks**: Lay out the blocks in your desired arrangement for the table runner. Play with color and pattern placement.

4. **Sew the Blocks Together**: Sew the blocks together in rows, then join the rows to form the complete table runner.

5. **Layer the Runner**: Cut a backing piece and batting to match the size of the finished top. Layer them with the crumb top, right side up.

6. **Quilt the Table Runner**: Quilt as desired, either with straight lines or free-motion designs.

7. **Bind the Edges**: Trim excess batting and backing, then apply binding around the edges to finish.

Crumb Quilt Wall Hanging with Applique

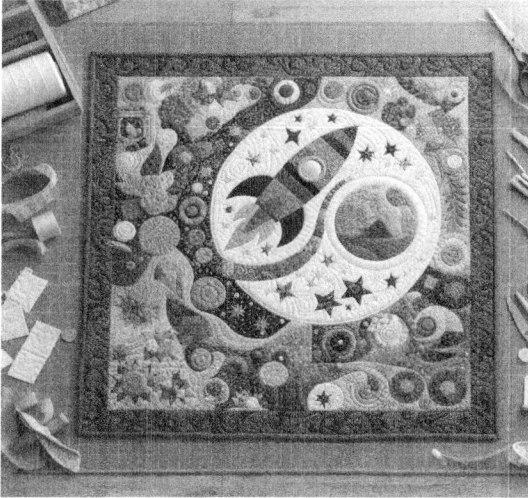

Materials Needed:

1. Fabric scraps (various sizes)
2. Background fabric (for the wall hanging)
3. Appliqué fabric (for shapes)
4. Fusible web (optional)
5. Thread (matching or contrasting)
6. Sewing machine

7. Rotary cutter, cutting mat, and quilting ruler

8. Iron and ironing board

Steps:

1. **Create the Crumb Background**: Sew together fabric scraps to form a large block for the wall hanging, approximately 24" x 36".

2. **Prepare the Appliqué Shapes:**

Cut shapes from the appliqué fabric and adhere fusible web to the back (if using). Alternatively, you can pin the shapes directly to the crumb background.

3. **Arrange the Applique**: Position the appliqué shapes on the crumb background. Once satisfied, press to secure.

4. **Sew the Applique**: Use a zigzag or decorative stitch to sew around the edges of the appliqué shapes, securing them in place.

5. **Layer the Wall Hanging**: Cut backing and batting to match the size of the top. Layer them accordingly.

6. **Quilt the Layers**: Quilt through all layers as desired, either with straight lines or creative free-motion designs.

7. **Finish the Edges**:

Trim excess fabric and bind the edges to complete the wall hanging.

Crumb Quilt Baby Blanket

Materials Needed:

1. Fabric scraps (various sizes)

2. Soft backing fabric (flannel or minky)

3. Batting (optional, for warmth)

4. Thread (matching or contrasting)

5. Sewing machine

6. Rotary cutter, cutting mat, and quilting ruler

7. Iron and ironing board

Steps:

1. **Create Crumb Blocks**: Sew together fabric scraps to create several blocks, each measuring 8" x 8". Aim for at least twelve blocks.

2. **Trim the Blocks**: After piecing, trim the blocks to ensure they are uniform in size.

3. **Arrange the Blocks**: Lay out the blocks in a 3 x 4 grid or any arrangement you prefer for the baby blanket.

4. **Sew the Blocks Together**: Sew the blocks together in rows, then join the rows to form the complete top of the blanket.

5. **Layer the Blanket**: Cut the backing fabric and batting (if using) to match the size of the top. Layer them accordingly.

6. **Quilt the Layers**: Quilt the layers together using straight lines or free-motion designs, ensuring even distribution.

7. **Finish the Edges**: Trim excess fabric and bind the edges to finish the baby blanket.

Crumb Quilt Tote Bag with Pockets

Materials Needed:

1. Fabric scraps (various sizes)

2. Lining fabric (cotton or canvas)

3. Interfacing (for sturdiness)

4. Thread (matching or contrasting)

5. Sewing machine

6. Rotary cutter, cutting mat, and quilting ruler

7. Iron and ironing board

8. Straps (fabric or webbing)

Steps:

1. **Create Crumb Blocks**: Sew together fabric scraps to create two large crumb blocks (12" x 18" each) for the bag exterior.

2. **Prepare the Pockets**: Cut smaller crumb blocks (6" x 8") for inside pockets. Make at least two.

3. **Layer the Pockets**: Attach interfacing to the pocket pieces for sturdiness. Fold and press the pocket pieces.

4. **Sew the Pockets**: Attach the pockets to the lining fabric by sewing them in place at desired heights.

5. **Assemble the Tote**: Place the crumb blocks right sides together and sew along the sides and bottom, leaving the top open.

6. **Insert Straps**: Attach straps to the top edge of the bag, ensuring they are securely sewn.

7. **Finish the Tote**: Sew the lining to the top edges, then turn the tote right side out. Press and topstitch for a completed look.

Crumb Quilt Throw Blanket

Materials Needed:

1. Fabric scraps (various sizes)

2. Backing fabric (soft cotton or flannel)

3. Batting (for warmth)

4. Thread (matching or contrasting)

5. Sewing machine

6. Rotary cutter, cutting mat, and quilting ruler

7. Iron and ironing board

8. Binding fabric

Steps:

1. **Create Crumb Blocks**: Sew together fabric scraps to create blocks measuring 10" x 10". Aim for at least 20 blocks for a throw blanket.

2. **Trim the Blocks**: Trim each block to ensure uniform size and neat edges.

3. **Arrange the Blocks**: Lay out the blocks in a 5 x 4 grid or any arrangement you prefer.

4. **Sew the Blocks Together**: Sew the blocks together in rows, then join the rows to form the complete top of the throw blanket.

5. **Layer the Blanket**: Cut the backing fabric and batting to match the size of the top. Layer them accordingly.

6. **Quilt the Layers**: Quilt the layers together using straight lines, stippling, or creative free-motion designs.

7. **Finish the Edges**: Trim excess fabric and bind the edges to complete the throw blanket.

These intermediate projects will help you develop your skills further while providing beautiful and practical items for your home or gifts for loved ones. Enjoy your crumb quilting journey!

CHAPTER 7

Advanced project

As you become more confident in your crumb quilting skills, you can tackle advanced projects that involve intricate designs and techniques. Here are five advanced projects, complete with the necessary materials and step-by-step instructions.

Crumb Quilt Medallion Quilt

Materials Needed:

1. Fabric scraps (various sizes)

2. Background fabric (solid color)

3. Batting (optional)

4. Thread (matching or contrasting)

5. Sewing machine

6. Rotary cutter, cutting mat, and quilting ruler

7. Iron and ironing board

8. Binding fabric

Steps:

1. **Create the Center Medallion**: Begin by sewing fabric scraps to create a central block (approximately 18" x 18"). This block will serve as the focal point of your quilt.

2. **Prepare Borders**: Cut strips of background fabric and additional fabriscraps to create multiple borders around the medallion. Aim for widths of 2" to 5" for visual interest.

3. **Attach Borders**: Sew the first border to the medallion, pressing the seams outward. Continue to add borders, alternating between solid and crumb fabric, until the quilt reaches your desired size.

4. **Layer the Quilt**:
Cut backing fabric and batting to match the size of the top. Layer them accordingly.

5. **Quilt the Layers:** Quilt the layers together using creative designs—such as echo quilting around the medallion or free-motion quilting throughout.

6. **Bind the Edges**: Trim excess fabric and bind the edges to finish the medallion quilt.

Crumb Quilt with Curved Piecing

Materials Needed:

1. Fabric scraps (various sizes)

2. Background fabric (solid color or pattern)

3. Batting (optional)

4. Thread (matching or contrasting)

5. Sewing machine

6. Rotary cutter, cutting mat, and quilting ruler

7. Iron and ironing board

8. Curved piecing templates (optional)

Steps:

1. **Create Crumb Blocks**: Sew together fabric scraps to create blocks measuring approximately 8" x 8".

2. **Prepare Curved Pieces**: Use templates or freehand cut curved shapes from your crumb blocks. Ensure that the curves are smooth and evenly shaped.

3. **Sew Curved Piecing**: Carefully sew the curved pieces together, using clips or pins to help guide the fabric. Press seams to one side.

4. **Arrange the Layout**: Lay out your curved pieced sections along with additional crumb blocks to create an engaging design.

5. **Sew Sections Together**: Join all sections together, ensuring that the curves line up nicely.

6. **Layer the Quilt**: Cut backing fabric and batting to match the size of the top. Layer them accordingly.

7. **Quilt the Layers**: Quilt the layers using a combination of straight-line and free-motion quilting techniques.

8. **Bind the Edges:** Trim excess fabric and bind the edges to finish the curved piecing quilt.

Crumb Quilt with Inset Blocks

Materials Needed:

1. Fabric scraps (various sizes)

2. Background fabric (solid color)

3. Batting (optional)

4. Thread (matching or contrasting)

5. Sewing machine

6. Rotary cutter, cutting mat, and quilting ruler

7. Iron and ironing board

8. Additional fabric for inset blocks

Steps:

1. **Create Crumb Blocks**: Sew together fabric scraps to create a variety of blocks (6" x 6" or larger).

2. **Prepare Inset Blocks**: Cut smaller blocks from your additional fabric to be inset into your crumb blocks. Ensure they are evenly sized.

3. **Sew Inset Blocks**: Sew the inset blocks into the crumb blocks by creating a cut in the crumb block and inserting the smaller block, securing with a seam.
4. **Arrange the Quilt Top**: Lay out your completed blocks to create an interesting arrangement.

5. **Sew the Blocks Together**: Join the blocks together to form the quilt top.

6. **Layer the Quilt**: Cut backing fabric and batting to match the size of the top. Layer them accordingly.

7. **Quilt the Layers**: Use various quilting techniques to highlight the inset blocks and crumb blocks.

8. **Bind the Edges**: Trim excess fabric and bind the edges to finish the inset blocks quilt.

Crumb Quilt Landscape

Materials Needed:

1. Fabric scraps (various sizes, including natural colors

2. Background fabric (solid for sky)

3. Batting (optional)

4. Thread (matching or contrasting)

5. Sewing machine

6. Rotary cutter, cutting mat, and quilting ruler

7. Iron and ironing board

8. Fabric paints or markers (optional for detailing)

Steps:

1. **Plan Your Landscape**: Sketch out a simple landscape design, deciding where to use crumb fabric for elements like hills, trees, and clouds.

2. **Create the Background**: Cut a large piece of solid fabric for the sky, then sew fabric scraps to form hills or other landscape features.

3. **Piece the Landscape**: Assemble the background and foreground elements, ensuring that everything flows naturally.

4. **Add Details**: Use smaller scraps or fabric paints to add details like flowers, trees, or other features to your landscape.

5. **Layer the Quilt**: Cut backing fabric and batting to match the size of the top. Layer them accordingly.

6. **Quilt the Layers**: Quilt using straight lines for the sky and free-motion designs for the landscape features.

7. **Bind the Edges**: Trim excess fabric and bind the edges to finish the landscape quilt.

Crumb Quilt T-shirt Memory Quilt

Materials Needed:

1. Fabric scraps (various sizes

2. T-shirts (old or new, cut into squares)

3. Batting (optional)

4. Thread (matching or contrasting)

5. Sewing machine

6. Rotary cutter, cutting mat, and quilting ruler

7. Iron and ironing board

8. Backing fabric (soft cotton or flannel

Steps:

1. **Prepare T-shirt Squares**: Cut t-shirts into squares (12" x 12" or your desired size), ensuring to include interesting graphics or quotes.

2. **Create Crumb Blocks**: Sew together fabric scraps to create additional blocks (also 12" x 12").

3. **Arrange Your Layout**:

Lay out your t-shirt squares and crumb blocks in a grid pattern, mixing and matching as desired.

4. **Sew the Blocks Together**: Sew the squares together to form the quilt top.

5. **Layer the Quilt**: Cut backing fabric and batting to match the size of the top. Layer them accordingly.

6. **Quilt the Layers:** Quilt using straight lines or creative free-motion techniques, ensuring to emphasize the t-shirt designs.

7. **Bind the Edges**: Trim excess fabric and bind the edges to finish the memory quilt.

These advanced projects will challenge your skills and creativity, allowing you to explore different techniques and designs within crumb quilting. Enjoy the process and the beautiful outcomes!

Troubleshooting and Solutions in Crumb Quilting

Even the most experienced quilters encounter challenges along the way. Here are common issues faced during crumb quilting, along with practical solutions to help you overcome them.

1. Uneven Seams

Issue: Seams may be uneven, leading to blocks that do not line up properly.

Solutions:

- **Use a 1/4" Seam Allowance**: Ensure you consistently use a 1/4" seam allowance for all seams. You can use a quilting foot with a guide or mark your sewing machine plate for accuracy.

- **Press Seams Open**: Pressing seams open rather than to one side can help reduce bulk and create a flatter block.

- **Check Machine Settings**: Make sure your sewing machine is correctly threaded and tension settings are appropriate. A well-threaded machine will produce cleaner stitches.

2. Fabric Bunching or Pleating

Issue: Fabric may bunch up or create pleats when sewing, especially when working with curved pieces.

Solutions:

- **Pin or Clip Fabric**: Use plenty of pins or fabric clips to secure layers while sewing. This helps prevent shifting.

- **Sew Slowly:** Take your time when sewing curves. Slowing down allows you to guide the fabric more effectively.

- **Use a Walking Foot**: A walking foot helps to evenly feed multiple layers of fabric through the machine, reducing bunching.

3. Poor Alignment of Blocks

Issue: Blocks may not align properly, resulting in a misaligned quilt top.

Solutions:

- **Double-Check Layout**: Before sewing, double-check the layout of your blocks. Use a design wall or floor space to visualize the arrangement.

- **Sew in Rows:** If you're making a quilt top from multiple blocks, sew the blocks into rows first, and then join the rows together for better alignment.

- **Square Up Blocks**: Use a rotary cutter and ruler to square up blocks after piecing. This helps ensure uniformity.

4. Fabric Fraying

Issue: Edges of fabric scraps may fray during handling or sewing.

Solutions:

- **Use Fray Check**: Apply a fray-check solution to the edges of fabric scraps before sewing.

- **Stay Stitch Edges**: Run a stay stitch (a straight line of stitching) along the edges of blocks to prevent fraying.

- **Choose Durable Fabrics**: Use fabrics that are less prone to fraying, such as quilting cotton, and avoid lightweight or delicate fabrics.

5. Difficulty in Free-Motion Quilting

Issue: Trouble maneuvering fabric during free-motion quilting, resulting in uneven stitches.

Solutions:

- **Practice**: Spend time practicing free-motion quilting on scrap fabric to build your confidence and control.

- **Lower Feed Dogs**: Ensure your machine's feed dogs are lowered to allow for free movement of fabric.

- **Use the Right Foot**: A darning foot or free-motion quilting foot can help you navigate better.

6. Inconsistent Tension

Issue: Inconsistent stitch tension can lead to puckering or loose stitches.

Solutions:

- **Check Tension Settings**: Make sure your sewing machine tension settings are appropriate for the fabric you're using. Adjust as needed.

- **Use Quality Thread**: Low-quality thread can cause tension issues. Opt for good quality quilting thread.

- **Test Stitches**: Always do a test stitch on a scrap piece of fabric before beginning your project to ensure proper tension.

7. Color and Pattern Imbalance

Issue: The quilt top may have an imbalance in color or pattern, making it visually unappealing.

Solutions:

- **Color Wheel**: Use a color wheel to help select complementary or contrasting colors for your blocks.

- **Step Back**: Periodically step back from your work to view it from a distance, which can help identify imbalances.

- **Use a Design Wall**: Arrange blocks on a design wall before sewing them together to get a better sense of balance and flow.

8. Difficulty with Binding

Issue: The quilt binding may be difficult to apply or not lay flat.

Solutions:

- **Cut Binding Strips Consistently**: Ensure that your binding strips are cut evenly, typically at 2.5" wide.

- **Sew Binding on the Bias**: If your quilt has curves, consider cutting binding on the bias for better flexibility.

- **Press Binding in Half**: Press binding strips in half before attaching them to help it lay flat and make it easier to sew.

With these troubleshooting tips and solutions, you'll be better equipped to handle common issues in crumb quilting. Remember that quilting is a journey of learning, and each challenge presents an opportunity to improve your skills. Happy quilting!

Conclusion

Crumb quilting is a delightful and liberating form of quilting that allows you to create beautiful, one-of-a-kind pieces using fabric scraps and your imagination. Throughout this guide, we've explored the history, techniques, and materials necessary for both beginners and advanced quilters alike.

By embracing the principles of crumb quilting, you not only produce unique quilts but also practice sustainability by repurposing fabric scraps that might otherwise go to waste. Each project, whether a simple block or an intricate design, offers the chance to express your creativity and showcase your personality.

As you embark on your crumb quilting journey, remember that every quilt tells a story. Whether you're working on beginner projects or challenging yourself with advanced techniques, take the time to enjoy the process and celebrate your progress. Don't be discouraged by mistakes; instead, view them as part of your learning experience.

With the tips and techniques outlined in this book, you are now equipped to tackle a variety of crumb quilting projects with confidence. May your quilting endeavors bring you joy, relaxation, and a deeper appreciation for the art of quilting. Happy stitching!

Printed in Great Britain
by Amazon